VISIBLE

VISIBLE

A WOMAN'S GUIDE TO *Unleashing* YOUR
FULL POTENTIAL IN THE WORKPLACE

LAURA ARROYO

ISBN: 978-0-578-97170-4
ISBN: 978-0-578-74018-8 (eBook)

For women like my mother, my grandmothers, my first woman boss, my tribe, my squaddd, my Fraternity, and the men who want to work with us.

*"In line at the drugstore it's finally your turn, and then it's not as he walks in front of you and puts his things on the counter. The cashier says, "Sir, she was next. When he turns to you he is truly surprised."
"Oh my God, I didn't see you."
"You must be in a hurry, you offer."
"No, no, no I really didn't see you..."*

*Citizen: An American Lyric
by Claudia Rankine, 2014*

CONTENTS

Introduction: PHD in Common Sense   *ix*

The Role Model You Needed   *1*

Missed Opportunities   *7*

Lucky You   *15*

The Power of 'Yes'   *23*

The Business of Boundaries   *33*

Mastering the Ego   *42*

Mind Your Manners   *50*

It's a Heart Thing   *58*

Bold and Brandable   *66*

Zero Talent   *73*

Challenging Collaborations   *78*

The Good Fight   *85*

Resisting Resilience   *91*

Sorry, Not Sorry   *98*

Definitions   *106*

Epilogue   *111*

Acknowledgments   *114*

"She made the mistake of raising me to have a voice."

—*Melissa Grushetski*

PH.D. IN COMMON SENSE

I was born in Hampton and raised in Newport News, Virginia, to a strict Hispanic immigrant mother. There isn't much difference between Hampton and Newport News, Virginia. In fact, they are so close that some people's front porch is in Newport News, and their back porch is in Hampton.

When I was seven years old, my mother insisted that Newport News would provide her three children, born three years apart, some haven from the dangers of Hampton. They have always been the same to me, but I am sure the government assistance Newport News would grant our family was a major motivating factor. We were a troop, the three of us. My two older brothers and I were goofy, fearless, and adventurous. We were a product of our neighborhood for sure. It has always been interesting to share my experiences from my childhood with my peers. I have discovered throughout the years that I grew up much quicker than any of them. The way I was raised compared to their sheltered and protected homes made me realize how different my home was. It is the wave an impoverished upbringing that you realize no one else around you experienced.

"So, you mean to tell me you have never hitch hiked?!"

These small seemingly insignificant moments in my life shaped my view of the world. By the time I was nine, I walked to the store often all by myself. As I walked into the store, I would go right to the candy aisle where Now and Laters, more affectionately called "*Nahlaeders*" by the children in the neighborhood, awaited me. Back then they were only about 10 cents each. I could find two nickels in the playground sand by the end of the week with no problem. This was the only way to make a candy run. God knows my mother was not going to give me money to get candy. I had to teach myself how to find change in unsuspecting places without being a crook or dishonest. I would always luck up somehow.

I taught myself many things like how to swing on a swing by initiating a rocking motion, shifting my weight back and forth until I got some air movement. Once I was in the sky, I realized I would need to learn how to make myself stop, so I went for it one day by springing my body out of the leather holster held by chains. I flew through the air and across the sand park in a craze.

I felt like superwoman.

I also played in dirt. Although getting good and dirty was one of the most fun moments of freedom and adventurous expression in my life, it seemed to be a point of contingency for my mother. My mother warned me of the spanking that awaited me if I brought lice home. My hair was made of big, long, dark brown locks of curls. I had more hair than it appeared my head could manage, so both children and adults alike often grinned over me in fascination with "Can I touch it?" fingers.

As a child, I feared the older children on the see-saw as they would try to "cherry bomb" us by putting all of their weight on one side of the seesaw while our legs flailed in the air on the other side. They would then jump off the seesaw causing all of our body weight to come crashing down. They would have a little mercy on me because I was a *girl* and could not handle the fear nor potential bruised butt that I would have the minute I would hit the ground. I got splinters deep down into my bottom and runs in my stockings. I tripped and fell hard on concrete, got mud on my face, and always smelled like grass and sweat, also known as "outside", my mother would say. That is where we grew up, outside.

When we were not at home, my mother dragged us around with her day and night. We simultaneously learned the Spanish and English language. Most people may have found that to be problematic, but while my mother only had a high school public education, she had a doctorate degree in common sense. Education was important in our household. We were held to high standards even if she could not meet them herself. Ironic, right? She didn't want us to be "othered". My mother did not want people to look at us stereotypically. After all, we were only visitors in this country. I was always told to "stay in a child's place". Little did she know, she was preparing us for a systemic battle that would be one of the most challenging fights of our lives.

I will never forget the day my mother purchased her first car. It was my 5th birthday. After a short bus ride home from school, the bus driver arrived at my stop. As I was getting off, the driver turned to me with a box of goodies. She said, "Happy Birthday Laura!" as she pointed to the box. I was allowed to take one item to celebrate. There were candy and toys in there. My eyes filled with excitement as I reached for an orange beaded necklace, but then I saw a piece of candy. I was so tempted to ask if I could take two items, but I knew I could never embarrass my mother with my greed. I would not dare step out of bounds as a child. I was afraid of adults, any form of authority, or a person who was superior to us. This fear caused me to be an introverted and quiet child. I never really spoke up for myself or challenged the norm.

I settled.

I settled for the orange beaded necklace, said thank you, and pranced off the bus. As I ran home from the bus, my mom awaited me at the door. She looked excited. My mother was never in a good mood, so this meant something special was happening. Her grin was warm and inviting. From what I recall, she told us to follow her outside. I skipped behind her as she walked to the parking lot. There it was, her not-so, brand-new, navy-blue station wagon. She was beaming with pride, and I was nothing short of elated. I could not believe my mother got us a car. I do not know how she did it, but she did. My mother always worked hard, so I know she earned every bit of this accomplishment. Her ambition to make our lives easier was admirable. It was not the best car, but it still is my favorite car.

My mother was tough, but she offered very little run-of-the-mill guidance. However, what she did provide, in my opinion, was far more valuable than traditional lessons most children learn from their parents. My mother taught me resilience, the will to overcome any obstacle I face, and the fierceness to show up for myself. She taught me when and how to be *visible*. My mother is one of the many reasons I am writing this book. The grit she taught me growing up helped mold me into the competent and confident leader I am today. She is the reason I realized I did not have to compromise who I was or diminish from where I gained my knowledge. Success is about strategy regardless of your background and where or how you were raised. All that is required to be successful and have great leadership qualities is being fair to others, having unwavering love for yourself, and the will to work your ass off.

In my career, I have had the pleasure of teaching hundreds of eager and even seasoned learners how to develop their careers to eventually move into leadership positions. These principles are simple yet require you to better understand who you truly are at your core to make strategic career decisions. I am tired of seeing women, especially women of color, being pushed to the wayside, being invisible to our counterparts no matter how hard we work, and being overlooked for promotions, but I don't blame any of us for the circumstances that we have been through. We all have gone through a social conditioning that has made us docile at times, and even when we do speak up we are often misunderstood.

You don't need to be fixed or silenced in board rooms. This isn't a fix being a woman in the workplace book. This is a shared experience guide that can help us learn from the past to carry our light into our futures. This is us changing the landscape of a workforce led by us, fully capable and fully *visible*.

"One child, one teacher, one book, one pen can change the world."

—Malala Yousafzai,
Pakistani Activist for Female Education
UN Youth Assembly (2013)

CHAPTER 1

THE ROLE MODEL YOU NEEDED

I was an awful student in school. I hated doing home-work, but I took pleasure in learning and teaching. This enjoyment came from my humble upbringing. I was my mother's poor translator and fake best friend for most of my childhood. She would drag me around everywhere, from grocery stores to leasing offices. I would have to dispute receipts when the cashier got too handsy with the scanner and interpret complicated term agreements in front of intimidating White women who wore glasses. What 10-year old knows how to explain an APR rate to another adult? Yet there I was, coming in at 4 ½ feet tall with doe-like eyes and long, brown, puffy curly hair, learning what was a foreign language to me – "adulting." I was very intrigued by new information, my ability to catch on quickly to any concept, and the sense of responsibility and accomplishment that would come alive in me through teaching my mother the ways of the world. I would help bring understanding to what seemed complicated and impossible for her.

The responsibility to become a pseudo-adult this early in my life created much anxiety in me as a child. I remember having chronic stomach aches. I was always incredibly shaky, and I was highly sensitive. On the flip side, I felt an overwhelmingly rewarding feeling helping my mother navigate the world. Her enlightenment made me feel like I solved a case or completed a puzzle. I quickly became the voice of reason in my family as early as I can remember. I was the "smart," more logical child.

As much as I avoided homework, you would be surprised to find me in Honors and Advance Placement (AP) classes every year. I credit this back to my upbringing. My mother was impatient. She needed things to happen quickly, which required me to learn and teach even quicker. This need made me intuitive. It required me to be a problem solver and instinctual. It was always "get with the program," so my brain interpreted every interaction I had as a child as "sink or swim." I now view the world through that lens because of it.

Being intuitive and solution-based makes for an expert test-taker. Every year, no matter how poorly I did during the semester, I would do very well during standardized testing, which landed me in the "big dog" classes.

In my tenth-grade year, I found myself with a 24-year old, tall, attractive, Black, Honors English teacher, Ms. Erica. I still cannot believe how much impact she had on me at her young age. Reflecting back when I was 24 years old, I remember being a complete mess. I probably drank more beer than water and I was in a constant state of heartbreak over my ex-boyfriend. Ms. Erica probably thinks the same of herself, but she was so smart and so cool in my eyes. She was a Hampton University Alumna. She was brilliant, beautiful, and the smoothest teacher I had ever met. She was witty, and I was impressed by how she could keep up with a sarcastic group of 15-year-olds.

I have been writing since my fingers were strong enough to hold a pencil. It is something I have loved and enjoyed as early as I can remember. I didn't grow up around a group of people who would admit they were literary writers. We were sandbox kids. The writers I knew were rappers, and those dreams were so far beyond the 2-mile radius in my mind it was the equivalent of alien speech. Naturally, I never connected with my love of learning, education, and literature until I was in Ms. Erica's class. She encouraged all of us to write robust stories about our lives, even if they may have been too painful or vulnerable to think about, she would encourage us to use our imaginations. I learned the art of literature, but what I got most out of being in her class was how I wanted to carry myself as a professional, what I wanted to major in in college, and how important education is to free yourself from worldly restrictions.

LEVEL-UP TIP:

Be an inspiration.

Aim to inspire others in the same way you have been inspired.

Have you ever heard the quote, "Be the person you needed when you were younger"? Many of us grew up without role models, mentors, and even positive parental figures. The true representation of what growing up in disenfranchised communities is like has always been misleading in media and on television. Our communities are often represented on the side of misfortune and lack of education. Still, the reality is our neighborhoods are rich in culture and collaboration, and we are thirsty for knowledge and information. Our neighborhoods are creative and innovative and we find ways to make "something out of nothing". I will never forget one of my neighbors created a flip book of illustrations that he designed entirely on his own. If you flipped the pages rapidly, you could see a figure drawn by a pencil come alive on the pages. We all wanted to get a hold of the book after he rounded us up to watch his "demo".

We did not have many role models or people to look up to around my neighborhood when I was younger. It was not because no one was willing, but because no one showed us how to be anything other than the images that flashed back at us on the television despite our various interests. With so much information at our fingertips today and our ability to become anyone we imagine ourselves to be. It is important to inspire others and be the people we needed when we were younger.

I desperately needed someone who looked like me and had the same interests as me to show me what was possible. I wasn't the brightest student, but I was motivated to write great stories and eventually share those stories with my community. That is why Ms. Erica is such an intricate person in my story. Ms. Erica opened my eyes to something I never really imagined. She was the perfect example of success, wit, and beauty. She had a love for teaching others, writing stories, and she was unapologetically black.

"Chances are you have business cards lying around from people you have met that are doing what you want to be doing who can help you - if you ask"

—Germany Kent,
American Author and Broadcast Journalist
The Hope Handbook: The Search for Personal Growth
(2015)

CHAPTER 2

MISSED OPPORTUNITIES

I decided to move out of my parent's home at the tender age of seventeen years old. It was not an easy decision to make. I had no idea what I was doing, but I knew I needed to get away from Virginia and my mother. My brother was already planting his feet in the bustling streets of Baltimore, MD, so he thought it would be a good idea for me to move in with him. We could help each other out. He was nineteen years old at the time and, like me, just as clueless. We were a team of sorts. There were nights that I could only afford a dinner that consisted of a bag of salt and vinegar chips and an Arizona Iced Tea. I will never forget pleading with the clerk at a gas station to scan my gift card one more time just to see if I had $1 on it so I could use the gas fumes to coast to my apartment. Our landlord had HVAC problems, so we often slept with the oven door open. Since we were so young, we never complained. Since we came from humble beginnings, we never felt we had the right to. The increased stressed made us fight all the time, but we loved each other, and we served as the support system we never knew we needed. My experience living with my brother is what prepared me for living as an independent adult.

During my years in Maryland, I successfully secured an Associate of Liberal Arts degree from the Community College of Baltimore County. I attempted a Bachelor of Arts in English Literature with a focus in Secondary Education from the University of Maryland, Baltimore County. The keyword here is attempted. I worked tirelessly for my degrees. I was going to work at a full-time job all morning and going to school all night. I faced endless financial hardship, totaled my mother›s car, and went through an insufferable breakup (twice...with the same person).

Through all of this, I managed to land a job with a non-profit organization that provided mental health services for families. The organization received a $5 million federal grant that would allow us to create a state-of-the-art training program for workers who served children and families. I was twenty-five years old when I started working there, making close to $45,000 a year, and my salary grew year by year. Not to mention, I traveled around the country, learned all there was to know about instructional design, marketing, system implementation, and evaluating facilitator-led and e-learning training courses.

I grew a keen interest in adult learning and employee development. It brought me back to that feeling I would get teaching my mother something new. Regardless of all the new information, they were pouring into me in this role; I will share several occurrences that gave me a feeling that I hit a glass ceiling at the organization. I wanted to be more than just an assistant. I was severely underutilized. I also knew deep down inside that I was worth more than what they were offering. I knew I would never be a member of management within the organization, so I started looking for other jobs.

LEVEL-UP TIP:

Trust your intuition.

When you feel that first shift in your spirit that suggests you are worth and capable of more than what you are currently experiencing, pay attention.

It wasn't long before I found myself applying for another non-profit organization in Bethesda, MD. Bethesda is an affluent community, where people with stuffy noses and subtle cologne thrive. I had several interviews with various key players within the organization. I hit it off with every single one of them. They loved me! The Bethesda non-profit offered a salary of $60,000 a year, along with a generous benefits package. I was over the moon.

When I got back to my current job, I opened my email to find a message from the director of human resources telling me the Bethesda non-profit was interested in hiring me. I could barely breathe as I read through her excitement. My next steps were to go through their online portal to complete a background check. I thought to myself, ok, sure, no problem. I slowly typed field by field, completing all sections concisely. I got to the education section, took a deep breath, and entered the graduation date I always used. I hit the submit button at the bottom of the page, and a sudden flush of nervousness overcame me.

The truth is, I walked across the stage, but I never completed my program. I was two classes shy of receiving my bachelor's degree, but I couldn't because of funding and lack of time. I closed my eyes as I shut down my computer and sighed. The next morning, I opened an email from the Bethesda, Director of Human Resources that read:

Good Morning Laura,

When we ran your background check, there was no record of a bachelor's degree at the University of Maryland, Baltimore County. Sometimes our system can glitch and fails to capture all necessary information. If you don't mind, could you send us your sealed transcripts?

Thank you,
Debra F., Director of Human Resources

Of all the companies that I interviewed and worked for, everyone has asked for a graduation date, but none of them verified completion.

I was mortified.

I missed an opportunity of a lifetime and thought maybe I would never come across another opportunity like this again. I sent an email to Debra, thanking her for her time and let her know I wanted to withdraw my application. She accepted my withdrawal and, as I can imagine, she was confused, but moved quickly to the next candidate.

I was bitter after this experience. I couldn't believe I was allowing myself to "just get by" for the past two years. I got too comfortable with the idea that I was gaining employment wherever I wanted without professional accountability. I was not honest with myself, and in many ways behaving with a sense of entitlement.

The next year, I decided to accept the good and bad and focus on the elements of my life I could control. I let go of my bitterness and got down to business. I embraced my journey and what was to come. Despite knowing it would be difficult, I made sure to love myself and all the parts of myself that I once viewed as "flawed."

I spent every ounce of my time dedicated to completing my bachelor's program. I borrowed money from my grandmother to free up the holds on my accounts. I requested a special schedule from my employer, read the research, wrote the papers, and spent countless sleepless nights completing some of my best work.

LEVEL-UP TIP:

Don't be afraid to ask for help.

There will be moments in your life where you drop the ball. Don't let those moments define you. The truth is that it is very little you can accomplish without strong relationships. Utilize those relationships to pick up the pieces when you have bitten off more than you can chew. I thank God for my grandmother, but for you, it might be a teacher, a peer, or a sibling. Swallow your pride and ask for help.

There are times we may feel like we have dug ourselves into a hole, and just the thought of going back to address it is the reason we never do. I never thought I would go back to finish my degree because it was too overwhelming to think it was possible. I owed the school thousands of dollars, and I knew the classes I needed would impact my work schedule. It all seemed impossible. When you find yourself in a hopeless situation, make sure you give yourself some grace. Make sure you forgive yourself for the opportunities you missed. Put one foot in front of the other every day. Remember to ask for help. Remember, the worst a person can say is "no." Once you've come out on the other side, remember to tell yourself, never again.

Diplomas don't have grades on them. They also don't have start dates on them. In the Fall of 2017, I received a Bachelor of Arts in English Literature. 6 years from when I first stepped foot on campus. There is nothing that makes me prouder.

"I am not lucky. You know what I am? I am smart, I am talented, I take advantage of the opportunities that come my way and I work really, really hard. Don't call me lucky. Call me a badass."

—*Shonda Rhimes,*
Award Winning American Television Producer and
Screenwriter; Grey's Anatomy, Scandal, and Private Practice

CHAPTER 3

LUCKY YOU

I sat at the end of our conference room table as five of our department directors looked on in disappointment—some off into the distance and others down at their note pads. The executive director just announced one of our honorary speakers for our 2015 Annual Gala relapsed into alcoholism.

Our Annual Gala brought in well over $200,000 each year in private donations from stakeholders and families directly impacted by the work we did every day, providing mental health support for families across the world. Our staff consisted of twenty intense, confident, opinionated mental health workers and support staff—all women. We made mountains move in that building, often working more than sixty hours a week to create state-of-the-art programming with little money and resources. Our clashing of personalities, coupled with the urgency of our shared goals, made us subtly hostile at times.

Tony was a young adult who relied on programs like the one our organization created to support the well-being and stability of children with nowhere to turn but the streets. He was our success story for a program we worked strenuously to stabilize. He was thrilled to learn he was selected to speak at such a prestigious event.

Just two months shy of the event, Tony had a "minor slip-up, not a full-blown spiral" into his past world of alcohol addiction and homelessness, his mentor explained.

It didn't matter.

Once the executive director learned of the episode, we knew this was a discussion we needed to have with our management staff, our board, and stakeholders. We were an organization built on values, full transparency, accountability, and intense love and support.

Our executive director explained the circumstances surrounding Tony's "minor slip-up" while posing the question, "What stance are we to take on this mishap?" Tony was supposed to be our standout guest, beating the odds, not becoming another statistic or number in the system. He was going to speak out to the crowd of over two hundred attendees to let them know about his success and how our program and funding helped him overcome some of life's most brutal challenges.

Though the truth of the matter was he made a wrong turn, and our program didn't help, and he didn't have the testimony he once had. The directors were all heartbroken, bitter, and disappointed. The compassion we preach every day needed to be proven in this moment, and our hands were tied. The leadership team went back and forth for a little while, and conclusively all agreed that we did not want to misrepresent our great organization by allowing him to share a bogus story. After all, what would Tony say? How will he represent our brand with his most recent relapse into the addiction that our organization was supposed to rescue him from?

After several minutes of discussion, one of the directors hesitantly introduced the idea of revoking his invitation altogether. Our invitations featuring his beaming smile already went out, so if Tony showed up that night, would our attendees question why we were not going to honor him? Would our integrity be in question?

As a non-profit organization, our funding and stability relied entirely on federal grants and funding from generous families. Most of the attendees would be donors and have the right to ask questions about our programming. The directors were trying to be mindful and stay ahead of any potential backlash. Some agreed to allow him to attend while others, hurt by the whole fiasco, were adamant that he did not deserve a second chance. I sat at the end of the table, shaking my head, increasingly becoming furious at the idea that we would revoke his invitation. After all, our organization was rooted in mental health services and therapy, and our fundamental ideals were founded on the idea of second chances.

I shook my head and sputtered through the strong voices in the room, barely audible. I was about to say, "I don't think what we are saying is fair-" but before I could get the words out of my mouth, our executive director slapped the table.

It startled everyone, but it shook me. She then looked at me and mouthed, „Shhhhh!". As if I were a child that needed disciplining. She did not say anything else at that moment, but her message was unmistakable. I was not there to speak. I was only there to scribe what the team was discussing. It crushed me. It felt as if she made me partially human, taking away my opinion, free thoughts, agency, and strengths. I knocked right back into my childhood. I was reminded at that moment, "Laura, you are only a visitor here. Don't you dare step out of bounds".

I worked as an administrative assistant for the organization for at least a year when I was asked to join the weekly management meetings to take notes and assist the organization with strategic planning efforts. Mostly, I was there to keep the management group organized. I was thrilled to be asked to join in on these meetings. Over the years, I had become extremely interested in organizational and business development. I knew I wasn't being brought in as the expert by any means, but I didn't think I would be silenced.

Two years before the «slap the table» incident occurred, I led a team of five Certified Alcohol and Drug

Counselors that administered a 12-Hour Early Inter-vention Alcohol Education Program. I was grateful to understand the needs of the people we served but mostly determined to grow the business. By the time I left the company, I had opened five additional locations, devel-oped two new programs, and worked diligently every day to discover new business development opportunities. I was a young woman in the workforce, but I served as a sponge for the leaders I admired: the ones who made the most sense, the ones who treated me with decency and respect.

LEVEL-UP TIP:

Recognize your worth.

Just because others cannot see your worth does not mean that it does not exist. You are the seer and determiner of the price fo your value.

At this point in my career, I thought very highly of myself and wanted my opinions to be valued. I had great things to offer any organization, and I had great plans to. It was amazing how, in an instant, my boss slapping the table, ordering me to shut up, stripped me of those feelings, and the confidence I developed for myself. It was a moment in my career that I would never forget. It propelled me into what I now know and understand to be extreme, "Imposter Syndrome."

LEVEL-UP TIP:

Understanding Imposter Syndrome

Imposter Syndrome is the psychological pattern in which one doubts one's accomplishments and has a persistent internalized fear of being inadequate despite record success. Imposter syndrome is what can keep us invisible in the workforce. We tend to shrink ourselves to protect and avoid hyper exposure, but it does the opposite.

Many of us have it, many don't even know we have it, but it is prevalent in high achieving minority women. No matter how many times you have proven to yourself and others that you are intelligent, a subject matter expert, and competent, you still find yourself feeling like you are not good enough, undeserving, merely an actress, or in a dream, or worse; just lucky.

It took some unlearning over the years to convince myself that luck has nothing to do with my accomplishments. After I left the organization, I vowed to never allow myself to devalue my work. Whenever you have something valuable to contribute to a conversation, share it without fear. The most important thing for your career is to own your successes and stand confident in your expertise. You put in the time. You put in the work. You are the expert. You are powerful. Nobody can take that away from you. Do not let anyone attempt to make you feel "grateful" for receiving crumbs at a table where a feast is available. You belong here too.

"Stop saying 'no' to everything and start saying 'yes.' What's the worst that can happen? A bit of embarrassment, a bit of awkwardness. And what's the best that can happen? You might meet some interesting people, have some new experiences, enjoy yourself."

—Sarah Haywood,
UK-British New York Times Bestselling Author
The Cactus (2018)

CHAPTER 4

THE POWER OF 'YES'

I decided to move to North Carolina after I received my bachelor's degree. I had a dear friend there, and quite frankly, I was miserable in Maryland. My brother moved back to Virginia, and I didn't have the same network of friends I once had when I was at the University of Maryland. The only thing I had to sustain me professionally and socially was my job. At this point in my life, I was willing to sacrifice my livelihood, all that I had learned, and the life I built for myself in Maryland to pursue possibility. If there was ever a time to do it, I had to do it now. I did not have any ties to anything.

To jumpstart my new life, I began to apply for work in North Carolina but found the cost of living was drastically lower than it was in Maryland. Naturally, wages were much less as well. I was overqualified and even having to turn down many opportunities due to unjustifiable salaries. I thought if I couldn't meet my salary requirements, I should at least pursue my passion; writing. I began working as a staff writer for pop-culture, current events website xoNecole.com, other media outlets, and I also created my own platform, LadyLaura.co, while looking for work. Many women have asked me how I got the opportunity to work for xoNecole.com, a major online publication. After all, we are talking about a Will Packer Media entity. My answer to this question is fairly simple. I will title this season of my life, "One Yes." After going on several interviews resulting in being overqualified and underpaid. I thought to myself, "they just don't understand what I'm capable of." All I need is for one person to say, "yes".

I decided to start inquiring and taking more chances in general. One day I began thinking about different ways I might be able to stand out as a contributing writer. I used my own platform, LadyLaura.co to pen an open letter to the editors at xoNecole.com or anyone who would listen.

The letter was titled, *Taking Chances: Letter to xoNecole:*

Good Morning,

An acquaintance of mine mentioned me under the comments section of your ad calling for contributors. I am ecstatic, 1) because my friend thinks I'm a good enough writer to contribute to the xoNecole brand, but 2) because I have been following the brand for a while and have seen how it has evolved. Like most women, we grow. Like most women writers, our content changes with that growth.

I am Laura Arroyo. I grew a passion for writing at a very young age. At first using it as a means for escape from my daily trials. You know, the ones that come with being a woman, and being colored, and having big hair and a radiant wild heart. I drew influence from the books I read, and quoted authors over and over again in my head to get me through. I realized the impact of writing and literature once I realized that I wouldn't have made it without it. I decided to pursue a Bachelors in English Literature largely because it was something I enjoyed, but I also had a young English teacher who taught me so much about how you can be transparent in your writing without gutting yourself...

All it took was one heartbreak. I started LadyLaura.co in 2014. My high school sweetheart moved out and I lost all sense of myself. I began writing excerpts for the blog as an outlet, which turned into relationship advice, which turned into lifestyle tips, and so on.

I'm writing you today, not because I want to discontinue LadyLaura.co, but because I know what it is like to be a woman that is lost in her junk. I know what it feels like to be liberated. I know what it is like to find a site, an article, a journal that I felt like had all the answers. I would like to contribute to the peace, laughter, and liberation of readers across the country, and hope that I'll have that chance on xoNecole.

I signed off by including a few pitch ideas and thanked the reader for their time.

I didn't think anyone would read it, and even if they did, I didn't think it would move the needle. I forgot about it until I opened my email a few mornings later and saw an inquiry from my blog page from the editing manager at xoNecole.com. Even then, I thought she was just thanking me for the post and acknowledging my blog. It was one of those moments where I thought I would get the "keep working" nod. As I opened her message, all I could see was, "I fell in love with your writing." I wanted to melt into my seat, but instead, my eyes watered. I felt seen. I felt heard. I felt *visible*. For someone who operates under the guise of imposter syndrome, this opened up the world for me.

LEVEL-UP TIP:

Don't sell yourself short for lack of experience.

Research says if women don't feel 100% qualified for an opportunity, they'll say 'no.' Whereas if men feel 60% qualified for an opportunity, they say 'yes!'. Saying 'no' to opportunities due to fears of any kind can limit your leadership growth in detrimental ways. If you have any transferable skills, say 'Yes!"

I learned a lot about the power of yes during this season of my life.

To make ends meet, I also started working a part-time job at a gym called Baseball Rebellion. Parents from all over the world brought their children in for hardcore baseball lessons. Some parents just knew their kid would be the next "A-Rod," while others only hoped to create a little bit of structure and discipline in their child's life. At Baseball Rebellion, I worked as a receptionist, checking people in for their lesson. I could tell the minute I stepped foot into the building; it was a growing company. I later learned the first baseball lessons they ever taught were in a barn house. Now, they owned a 12,500 square foot state-of-the-art training center and a business that was continuing to grow year by year.

On a Thursday evening, the owner completed his final lesson around 9:30 PM. My role required me to stay until the last customer left the building to close the gym together. As I wiped down the front desk and shut down my computer for the evening, I became curious, watching the owner with his hands gently planted on his waist, walking around. We talked for an hour or two about business, marketing, and entrepreneurship.

> ## LEVEL-UP TIP:
>
> ### Seize opportunities to network with successful people.
>
> *Whether they work in the field you want to go into or not, successful people tend to have distinct characteristics that have helped them in their success. Very often, it has little to do with their business model and more to do with who they are as people. Listen and be open-minded to those gems.*

"How did you do it?" I asked. His response was simple. *"Every day, I just try to find ways to say, 'Yes.'"*

Saying 'yes' while working in service can be quite the feat. Anyone who has ever worked in customer service knows how annoying and entitled customers can be. I was shocked to learn this 6'3, 220lb guy who was on the verge of creating an empire had enough self-awareness to put his ego to rest when it came to his business. He found ways to say 'yes' to his customers every single day. He made accommodations for scheduling, personally responded to pressing concerns, and made his clients feel like they were his very first client with every interaction.

My stint at the Baseball Rebellion was not long at all. Of course, I wasn't breaking any banking systems with my salary as a receptionist there, but it didn't matter to me. I truly enjoyed working with those gentlemen. They worked around odd schedules, weird children, and, worst of all, their parents. The staff at Baseball Rebellion always accommodated me and never made me feel uncomfortable in such a heavily male-dominated field. The team cultivated relationships by consistently saying 'yes,' as often as possible.

I read a quote on Twitter a while ago that read, *"never burn long term bridges for short term hunger, the crumbs never taste as good as the loaf."* It reminded me of the importance of finding ways to 'yes' and cultivating healthy relationships. The managing editor at xoNecole. com didn't have to say yes to anything. She didn't owe me anything, but she saw the power in building a relationship with a wonderful writer who had a lot to contribute to the platform.

Naturally, I thought it was impossible to say 'yes' to everyone. I thought, "you wouldn't be in business very long." There is no way possible you can please everyone's every need. It reminded me of an episode in the third season of Bob's Burgers, "Lindapendent." The mom character on the show, Linda, takes up a job at a grocery store. Due to Linda's giving and almost doormat-like nature, Linda ends up unconsciously letting all of her employees take the day off, leaving her alone at the grocery store. She becomes too overwhelmed, so she ends up abandoning the chaotic store.

LEVEL-UP TIP:

Saying yes does not mean becoming a doormat.

Lead with 'yes' to the needs that serve you and the company, not others' personal needs. Check your choices against your inner compass. This is what prevents you from becoming a doormat.

There is no way anyone can continue to say 'yes' to everything without feeling overwhelmed or under-compensated. Many times, after observing and reflecting on how these gentlemen grew and sustained their business for this long, I discovered finding ways to say 'yes,' is not the same thing as saying 'yes' to everything. Saying 'yes' is more about compromise. It is about meeting in the middle, to ultimately work together.

One of the habits in Franklin Covey's bestselling book, 7 Habits of Highly Effective People, is to aim for win/win. This doesn't always mean that you must sell your soul. It means you must find ways for both parties to win. By doing so, you have a higher chance of winning others over to get what you want in the long run.

So, what is it about assurance and certainty that creates an environment for success? The past ten years before this moment, I said yes to every opportunity that crossed my path.

There wasn't a part-time job I didn't take…

a favor I didn't commit to…

a copy-write gig I didn't write…

a seminar I didn't listen to…

or a conference I didn't attend.

If it was available to me and made sense for my growth, I would say yes. I always knew that even when I had to make short term sacrifices, whether it was money, time, or effort, it would still benefit me in the long run, even if I didn't see an immediate return on my investment. I knew saying "yes" to others ultimately meant saying "yes" to myself. Someone else's "win" does not take away from my own "wins."

Today I am a successful author, talent professional, instructional designer, and small business owner. I would say this is impressive for someone who just turned 32 and has every strike against them.

Born to an immigrant mother.

Born in public housing.

Born a woman.

Born brown.

Born loud.

"I think I've realized that business and being polite don't match. You can be fair, but me being polite was not me being fair to myself."

—*Beyoncé Knowles Carter,*
Multi-Platinum American Vocal Artist,
Entertainer, and Entrepreneur

CHAPTER 5

THE BUSINESS OF BOUNDARIES

I was quietly listening to a friend talk about our current dating climate one afternoon when I realized the power of setting boundaries. She was going on and on with her list of "Don'ts" when getting to know someone, and my first reactive thought was, *"Wow, it is going to be challenging for her to find someone."*

The conversation we had that afternoon never left me, though, and I began to think about what it meant to say 'no' or decide that something is not for you. The truth is, although I have shared in previous chapters the importance of compromise, it is equally important to have firm, unblurred boundaries.

At first, I thought of my friend as too picky and intentionally difficult, but she was actually the opposite. She was very intentional and very efficient in relationship building. Over the years, I have learned being intentional with your boundaries and being firm in saying "no" allows us to own our voices. Being nice is not more important than having a voice.

In our society, women and our perceived persnickety ways receive frowns from our counterparts. More specifically, if you are a woman of color. I have seen it in action, and I have dealt with it myself. We have always been encouraged to take what we can get, and for decades we have stood by patiently waiting for what we believe we deserve rather than requiring what we know we are worth. The nature of our society makes us excuse unacceptable behavior in relationships and business alike. It seems like we are the ones who have to be flexible and forgiving.

Unfortunately, this has occurred to me in the more male-dominated industries I have worked. Still, I am fortunate enough not to have experienced the crossing of boundaries from any of my direct male bosses.

LEVEL-UP TIP:

Not all jokes are funny.

There are times men can make lighthearted commentary that can make us feel uncomfortable. If it's not funny, don't laugh. Be vigilant and highly self-aware of your predetermined personal and professional boundaries in male-dominated spaces. Make them clear to your counterparts with poise and precision.

I know this notion has some "Me Too" undertones, and while I'll address that issue as well, I want to discuss the more covert ways power lines become blurred.

(The "Me Too" movement was created "to empower women through empathy and solidarity through strength in numbers, especially young and vulnerable women, by visibly demonstrating how many women have survived sexual assault and harassment, especially in the workplace.")

In traditional professional workplace settings, some people can cross civil boundaries through the undermining of one's work, through challenging one's intelligence and professional expertise.

I scheduled a meeting with a few top managers in a company I worked for to inform them of our upcoming employee development programming plan for the year. It was an exciting opportunity for frontline managers to start thinking about organizational career development and planning for the future. I was thrilled! I gathered all of my documentation in preparation for this meeting. I knew they would have questions about the new program structure and benefits. Like with most companies, anything new brings on its own set of new anxieties.

I sat across the table with five men looking at me as I introduced the new program. I made it a point to set my expectations, ask for input, and made sure to compromise as challenges arose. I felt good at the end of the conversation. I gained their buy-in and felt supported in my new initiative.

As I was gathering my forms, the director of operations turns and looks at me and says in a high-pitched "girl-like" voice while batting his eyes and moving his head side to side, "Were we good listeners?". His question was snarky, insulting, and degrading in tone and patronizing language.

I was genuinely embarrassed, and it was extremely awkward. Per usual and like most women, I appeased him to make his remark seem less out of place and replied, *"Yes, you were, thank you for that,"* as I smiled through my clenched teeth. I made myself just as small as he was trying to make me. I cringe when I think of this moment. He crossed a power boundary by stripping away the value of what I had to offer the group. He reduced me to a little girl.

Over the past few years, I have understood what boundary-crossing looks like and how to become a lot less passive and more assertive in my approach to my peers. I have mastered the importance of having boundaries in the workplace and balancing my 'no' responses with a timely and appropriate 'yes' as previously shared. This more mature and evolved version of me would not have shrunk myself to accommodate anyone. That is a boundary I now have set for myself. We are not baby dolls. We are peers and should be treated as such.

Setting boundaries may be one of the most challenging things you will have to do in your career. After all, we as women have historically let people practically get away with murder thus far. Maybe you have never experienced an abuse of power in the way that I have experienced it, so I will give you another more common boundary-crossing experience in the workplace.

Someone may ask you to complete a task that you know you are not equipped for, passionate about, or you are just plain uncomfortable with the work being asked of you. Still, for the sake of being an easy-going team player or wanting to be perceived as agreeable, you choose to suffer through these uncomfortable, non-developmental tasks. More often than not, the daunting task becomes a part of your everyday role and responsibilities. Who is in the wrong here? Your boss for not knowing what makes you tick, or you for never letting them know?

LEVEL-UP TIP:

Speak up for yourself.

Take ownership of the responsibilities you say 'yes' to. It's not your boss's job to say no, it is yours. So, what are you allowing in your professional life by not speaking up for yourself?

By addressing your boundaries and challenges as soon as they arise, this skill and habit will allow you to set the standard for future delegation in the workplace. Compassion without boundaries often leads to self-betrayal.

You have to know when to challenge a situation you are uncomfortable with respectfully. Sometimes this means having hard conversations. Although hard discussions are trying for many people, they are what strengthens relationships. By addressing your boundaries as soon as someone crosses them, we, in turn, are setting expectations for how we would like to be handled by others, the work that we enjoy doing, and the work we do well.

Now back to, "Me too."

On a much deeper level, you may have encountered undesirable or inappropriate behavior at work. For the sake of office politics or fear of retaliation, you remained quiet, pretended something you experienced never happened, or worse; you joined the offender by laughing or making the inappropriate behavior seem small.

We recently witnessed the perfect example of this on a podcast called, "*See the thing is...*". There are three women who host this show on the Joe Budden Podcast network. On episode 16, Joe Budden sat in with the ladies and continued to make sexually suggestive remarks to one of the hosts, Olivia Dope. While watching the video back on YouTube, you can see her smile through her clenched teeth. As Olivia Dope accounts three months after the recording, his remarks made her extremely uncomfortable and fearful of dampening the mood if she did not laugh along while he made those sexual remarks to her. Olivia made the difficult decision to leave the podcast because she was traumatized and embarrassed after the episode aired.

After learning about this event through online chatter and blogs, I felt a deep sense of hurt for Olivia. Only women, and specifically women of color experience this sizing exercise from our counterparts. It is unfortunate that sometimes we must take the long route back to our offices to avoid contact with someone. It is unfortunate that we have to quit our jobs, our livelihood, our dreams in some cases to stop the bleeding of an uncomfortable environment. There is a performance women of color have to play into. We can never truly bring who we are to work because of our cautious clenched smile that holds our anxieties from seeping out.

After experiencing some pretty gross behavior in the workforce myself, I promised that I would never let anyone make me uncomfortable without speaking up for myself first.

A simple, yet firm, *"Hey, do you mind doing/not doing (insert behavior)?"* These words will signal to the offender that you do not appreciate their behavior, and you anticipate change.

By addressing issues as soon as they happen, you avoid those problematic and more significant conversations later. It is hard not to laugh awkwardly and be the person who evens out the tone in the room. It is in our nature to be that person, but no more. Your intention is not to be pegged as the "mean girl" at work or make your colleagues feel like they have to tiptoe around you, but once they know, they know. You'll never have to have that discussion again because as they were getting to know you, you already set your expectations of them.

There is a difference between being confrontational in a healthy way and in a combative way. Confrontation is meant to be constructive and to salvage the relationship for both parties. Combat means to be destructive, with no regard to future relations between those involved. Being firm and consistent is the way to go.

Everyone has a line. Establish what your line is early on to know how to deal with people who don't respect your boundaries. It isn't merely about being "picky" or "sensitive." It is about accepting what you can handle from others and understanding how your boundaries, or lack thereof, can impact your mental health and destroy your relationships. Often, we allow relationships to drain us to the point of no return because of our lack of boundaries.

"The ego hurts you like this: you become obsessed with the one person who does not love you. blind to the rest who do."

—Warsan Shire,
Writer, Poet, Editor, and Teacher

CHAPTER 6

MASTERING THE EGO

I have worked in many capacities throughout my career, but being a writer has been one of my favorite roles. I have read and written many articles surrounding the mental health and wellbeing of black and brown women. As I have grown in my career, I have analyzed our behaviors in the workforce at all levels and capacities. What I have learned along the way is the very thing we, as women of color, receive criticism for is what makes us ideal leaders of people. When we reposition ourselves and remove the burdens and conditioning of self-victimization and self-entitlement, we can thrive in ways that our counterparts cannot.

Many people in the workforce believe women are too emotional, too impulsive, too people-focused, and too bossy to lead or substantially impact strategic business development. Those people have got it all wrong. Your voice, your emotional IQ, and your ability to empathize with others is your superpower! In this book, you have stumbled upon a few suggestions on where shifts in your thinking may be required for you to level-up and grow into your true potential. But I assure you, this book›s intention does not encourage you to dim your light and the things that make you powerful and unique. Instead, it would be best if you walked away, knowing how to use your emotions in a strategic way to build presence and perform at a high level.

There is a fable that was written by Madhu Bairy titled, The Wind and the Sun. I would like to share it with you to give you a better analogy of what I mean by using your innate power.

"The North Wind and the Sun had a quarrel about which of them was the stronger. While they were disputing with much heat and bluster, a Traveler passed along the road wrapped in a cloak.

"Let us agree," said the Sun, "that he is the stronger who can strip that Traveler of his cloak."

"Very well," growled the North Wind, and at once sent a cold, howling blast against the Traveler.

With the first gust of wind the ends of the cloak whipped about the Traveler's body. But he immediately wrapped it closely around him, and the harder the Wind blew, the tighter he held it to him. The North Wind tore angrily at the cloak, but all his efforts were in vain.

Then the Sun began to shine. At first his beams were gentle, and in the pleasant warmth after the bitter cold of the North Wind, the Traveler unfastened his cloak and let it hang loosely from his shoulders. The Sun's rays grew warmer and warmer. The man took off his cap and mopped his brow. At last he became so heated that he pulled off his cloak, and, to escape the blazing sunshine, threw himself down in the welcome shade of a tree by the roadside."

If you noticed, the sun did not have to change who he was to be as persuasive and have influence over others. This is the exactly what I mean by using our abilities and divine feminine energy to motivate and have influential leadership.

Being more strategic makes you more open to seeing things from other perspectives. This causes us to be more aware of not only others but, more importantly, ourselves. When we realize that nothing will be given to us, people become attracted to our ability to have the audacity to get things done and our ability to show our value. Realizing your important piece to the puzzle by seeing others will help you determine what you need to do to be successful.

Taking hold of your life is nearly impossible and counterproductive if you do not control your emotions. As a woman, your ability to have a sharp sense of self-awareness and your ability to use all of what you have for the benefit of yourself and others is your gift of feminine influence. You shape your world and the world of others. Your emotions are directly connected to your being's subconscious parts that drive your life in a distinct, impactful way. This active, and at times inactive subconscious part of who you are is often referred to as – the ego. Be aware of its presence. Learning to master the ego will guide your life down a path of wisdom, self-control, and peace.

LEVEL-UP TIP:

Check your ego.

Your ego is an important tool you will use throughout your career. It plays a huge part in the way we think of ourselves, and it is most visible and activated in the workplace. By learning to manage your ego, women can quickly shift their mindset into different and more beneficial perspectives.

At times, we can allow our egos to get the best of us. In traditional circles with high achieving women, we can carry mindsets that enable us to believe we are above specific tasks or worth more than others. Other times, when our ego is too low, we might victimize ourselves and create nonexistent problems that do not allow us to be coachable for the greater good of the people we serve, the peers we work with, and the employees who work for us. Anytime we think too highly or too lowly of ourselves, our ego is at play and can be quite a distraction in our lives.

The magic occurs when women learn the ability to know when it is appropriate to connect to those driving emotions and how to set boundaries for disconnection when necessary. When our egos are out of control, others view us as impulsive or demanding, rather than knowledgeable and assured.

Receiving feedback is one instance that stirs our ego. Our lack of control causes this. When women are not in control of a situation, we might feel vulnerable. Vulnerability creates its own set of emotions in us, including fear, isolation, and insecurity. Feedback is an inevitable part of employment that we all face, so we must start to recognize the benefits of constructive feedback.

Regardless if your employer is being fair or recognizing your challenges, it is important to use all feedback as an opportunity to learn. Learning happens in all capacities. Putting yourself in the other person's shoes can make feedback more digestible.

It is important to listen to the other person's concerns. As much as we think we can multi-task, you cannot listen and talk simultaneously. Listen carefully. Listen intently. Once the person is done sharing their feedback, rather than jumping into a defensive mode, express what you understand about the feedback and what you are taking away from it. Coming to unemotional conclusions allows you to continue to be respectful and use the feedback to work in your favor. Also, you do not have to resolve everything immediately. Some conversations can be revisited once you have had more time to think about it. Focus on listening.

Although you might feel like you have lost your control over a situation, it's not true. You have control over your own narrative, how you respond to negative feedback is what you will be known for. I always tell women through my coaching sessions, never allow anyone to disrupt who you were created to be. If you are a loving person, give love. If you are a forgiving person, forgive. Just don't let anyone turn you into someone you don't want to be based on their own actions. You cannot control what other people do. However, you? You were wonderfully and carefully made. Never let anyone play you out of that position.

LEVEL-UP TIP:

Ask questions.

Focus on how you respond. Next time start by asking questions. Ask the person for clarifications or to repeat the feedback so that you understand. If the person is delivering bad feedback 9 times out of 10, they will see how silly they sound once it is repeated.

Don't get me wrong, nobody is perfect, and not everyone will make the right decisions, at the right time, all the time. As you begin to garner success, check on your sense of entitlement regarding your experiences and opinions of things. Also, check on the ways that you become entirely selfless and consistently put yourself on the back burner. Neither of these mindsets is beneficial to anyone. Instead, start thinking in terms of the "big picture" goals for yourself and what you have to contribute to the world. Once your mind shifts towards these objectives, you will realize that every moving piece is vital in completing a puzzle. Every role is critical to move one step forward to create an environment where people can thrive personally and professionally. Our workplaces should be conducive to the wellbeing and success of women.

Whether you are the person who dumps the trash out at night or a long-term stakeholder, you are valuable. No role is above you or beneath you. Act like it.

"I say ma'am and sir to my age contemporaries and open doors for anyone that I can. This goes for men, too, though it is appreciated when they beat me to it and disappointing when they don't."

—Tiffany Madison,
Journalist and Novelist,
Author of Black and White, (2008)

CHAPTER 7

MIND YOUR MANNERS

I was with an employer for a little over a year when a significant reorganization occurred at the vice president and director level of management. Naturally, I was nervous and very excited as two women accepted the vice president of human resources and director of learning and performance roles. I knew some significant changes were on the horizon as these fierce leaders dove in headfirst by studying the company's current status and culture.

As the changes began rolling in, I remembered an article my new boss sent me from The Harvard Business Review. The article was titled *Managing Oneself* by Peter F. Drucker. She thought it might be an exciting read for me. I was in the middle of piloting a new employee development program for eleven eager participants. I was thrilled to learn, not only had I been the employee chosen to create the programming, but this was also another opportunity for me to be visible and enhance my professional brand.

I read through the article, which discussed values, belonging, and how to determine where you can contribute to an organization. As I skimmed through the twelve-page document, I found a passage that read,

> *"Manners are the lubricating oil of an organization. It is a law of nature that two moving bodies in contact with each other create friction. This is as true for human beings as it is for inanimate objects."*

The article went on to state the following;

> *"Manners - simple things like saying "please" and "thank you" and knowing a person's name or asking after her family—enable two people to work together whether they like each other or not. Bright people, especially bright young people, often do not understand this. If analysis shows that someone's brilliant work fails again and again as soon as cooperation from others is required, it is probably indicating a lack of courtesy—that is a lack of manners."*

These few sentences were probably the most profound yet straightforward thing I read all year long. The line that struck me the most is that *"bright people, especially bright young people, often do not understand this."* I could not help but think of the thousands of women of color in the workforce who could benefit from merely using our best assets- our emotions, our soft spot, our innate concern for others' well-being.

It is in these moments that our superpower, feminine intuition, and emotional intelligence shines through. Our emotions bring balance, understanding, and vibrancy to an otherwise cold, linear, and dichotomous world.

Never forget the people you interact with every day have families, challenges, worries, and burdens just as much as anyone else. Have you ever sat at the dinner table and talked to your husband about a snarky comment your boss made that day? Or called a friend on your car ride home to vent about how things were going at work? The people you work with are no different from you, so don't think you haven't been the topic of a discussion in a dining room or a car ride conversation for one second.

Caring for others is one of your most significant and most valuable assets. Genuine concern for the well-being of others is what causes your light to shine through. If you can get people to like you, you will gain their cooperation, also known as buy-in.

LEVEL-UP TIP:

Consider the <u>needs</u> of your team.

Your inability to collaborate and consider your team will hold you back tremendously. After all, when a promotional opportunity comes along, who do you think your leadership will look to determine if you are qualified or a good fit for the new role? They will look to the people (your managers, individual contributors, and collaborators) you have worked within the past. If they can trust you with a little bit, they are more willing to trust you with a lot.

Now, I understand that some people at your workplace (or even in your social life) will spend 40-hours a week committed to misunderstanding what you say and who you are as a person. This is where you will need to bring in acute strategy and a sense of self-awareness. I know it is much easier to act like you don't care than to face the issue head-on. Acknowledge that the other party has the absolute right to feel however they choose about you professionally and personally. In turn, remember that you also have the right to self-validate your behaviors, knowing your heart and judgment are in the right place. Move forward without regard. Live your life fully. Make your decisions confidently. Stand by your word to honor others, purely. I want you to remember what Michelle Obama so graciously repeated throughout her time in the White House, "When they go low, we go high."

Winning over stubborn people is easy once you remove your ego, so here are a few ways to win over those select few people who are hell-bent on being your enemy.

Ask the person for help with something (even if you don't need the help.)

Asking someone for help elevates their expertise and singlehandedly tears down their ability to be passive-aggressive or unhelpful. Our brains cannot process doing something for someone or helping someone we dislike. Once you remove your ego, ask someone for assistance, even if it's for something trivial. A switch will go off in that person's head. After all, you have made them the subject matter expert. You have deemed them to be smart, needed, valuable. One of the first things I learned early on in my career is that people have to like you and enjoy working with you to get anything done. The brain game wins every time.

Manners are not solely for behaviors, but they are also necessary for how we address people.

As a millennial in the workforce, learn quickly who around you prefers to be called by a pre-fix like Mr., Sir,

Mrs. If you are unsure, don't second guess, do it anyway. Most people will let you know if they do not want to be called by a pre-fix.

Learn people's names, but more importantly, learn how to pronounce other people's names.
Do not be afraid to ask someone how to pronounce their name and let them know you want to make sure you get it right. This practice is essential and intentional. It shows that people are meaningful to you. I do this primarily out of respect for others, their culture, and humanity. You have no idea where people are from or what they have been through before arriving at your company.

LEVEL-UP TIP:

Treat the janitor with the same manners as you would the CEO

A good measurement of someone's real character is how they treat people who can't do anything for them. People are more inclined to acknowledge or straighten up when the CEO walks into the room. The reality is everyone deserves our full attention and acknowledgment.

People that feel respected tend to treat those who show them respect more favorably. They tend to be warmer, do more favors for you, and find ways to accommodate your needs because they feel like you see them as human beings rather than objects or barriers to what you are trying to accomplish.

Own up to your mistakes.

People who are not fair and honest cannot earn people's trust. If you make a mistake, the courteous thing to do is apologize. Apologizing shows more power than you might think. Your ability to live in your truth welcomes others to let down their guard to do the same. Vulnerability is one of our most powerful traits.

Likability has a lot to do with having simple manners. Take yourself back to the days our parents would tug on our small hands to acknowledge someone's presence by saying "hello" or whisper to us, say "thank you," or "excuse me." The reality is nobody in this world is too busy to be pleasant or well mannered. Even Beyoncé introduces herself when she walks into a room.

"Integrity is choosing courage over comfort, choosing what's right over what's fun, fast or easy, and practicing your values not just professing them."

—*Brene Brown, Ph.D., LMSW,*
American Social Worker, Professor, Author,
and thought authority on vulnerability and shame
Rising Strong: How The Ability to Reset Transforms the Way
WE Live, Love, Parent, and Lead (2015)

CHAPTER 8

IT'S A HEART THING

I was listening to a popular podcast when one of their co-hosts recommended reading a book about self-publishing. I always knew I wanted to write a book one day, but I had no idea that it would be about leadership and talent development. I had no idea I would find purpose in helping black and brown women succeed in the workforce. Still, as I grew in my career, it was a calling that I could not ignore. I would coach and mentor woman after woman, some young and old, and what stood out to me the most was the glaring lack of leadership support women of color received in disproportionate amounts. Shockingly, I most recently discovered that a person of color's college degree is often viewed as equal to a white person's high school diploma.

As I began writing and sharing accounts and experiences in a way I thought readers would enjoy, I realized that my writing required a higher level of vulnerability. My accomplishments, my trials, and all of my moments of uncertainty were not the easiest to communicate in words. Self-guidebooks can mirror journaling and diary entries because they offer personal, raw, and unfiltered advice. Being in this state can trigger subconscious parts of your brain that recall special and joyful moments. Still, they can also force us to recall painful experiences filled with shame and defeat.

As a woman of color, specifically a Latina, I realize that my life and experiences are different from the average professional in corporate America. My aesthetic and appearance, the neighborhood where I'm from, and my beliefs/ideologies have given me some disadvantages. However, from my perspective, I view them as divinely ordered, God-given gifts that give me the vantage point to win in my lane.

I knew the topic of gaining buy-in would be a required element of this guidebook because it is critical for mobility in one's career. Interestingly enough, I struggled to explain it. For weeks, I circled trying to find the perfect words to describe what it meant to gain buy-in. I wrote, I read what I wrote, I hated what I wrote, I deleted what I wrote, and I started from scratch more times than I would like to admit.

After taking some time off to reflect on why I was writing this book in the first place, I realized I was missing a critical point-of-view. Initially, I focused my writing efforts on describing professional development strategies, managing the nuances of office politics, and the science behind acquiring a supportive following within the workplace. It was boring. It wasn't me. It wasn't us.

This leadership thing is a heart thing.
The leaders we look up to and follow don't have some fancy secret to success, know more mathematical equations than you do, or have a universal remote to control everything around them. True leaders gain buy-in from the heart.

Leaders gain buy-in through their ability to be honest, trustworthy, courageous, and reliable. I know this because I have experienced it, but I found real research to back what I've always thought to be true in a witty, blonde-haired researcher named Dr. Brené Brown.

Dr. Brené Brown is an expert social worker with specializations in a better understanding of shame and vulnerability. I was listening to Oprah's Super Soul Conversations Podcast: The Anatomy of Trust one morning when I discovered Dr. Brown. Her many titles include but are not limited to professor, lecturer, author, and podcast host. Dr. Brown led a profound conversation on "The Anatomy of Trust." It hit me like a ton of bricks as I listened to her share some of her most vulnerable moments and how they relate to how we, fallible humans, begin to trust people.

One of the ways humans gain and lose trust is through breaches in moral integrity. Integrity, as defined by Dr. Brown, is "choosing courage over comfort, choosing what's right over what's fun, fast or easy, and practicing your values not just professing them."

Gaining buy-in is about earning the trust of others by doing what is moral and ethical consistently. Buy-in acquisition is less about impressing others and more about accomplishing your own goals while building a community of flexible allies to support you if the time arises.

As you walk in your daily life as a leader, you will learn simple ways to gain buy-in from your peers and the people you lead.

Honor your word

The first of many ways to do this is simply being a woman of your word. Don Miguel Ruiz, who wrote "The Four Agreements," discusses the importance of your word, the words you say, how you use them, and how you deliver on them. "Be Impeccable with Your Word," he shares because there is life in the tongue.

Don Ruiz writes, "How much you love yourself and how you feel about yourself are directly proportionate to your word's quality and integrity." Ultimately, the way you view and treat your word is how you feel about yourself. Regardless of whom you are speaking to, whether it be the housekeeper, boss, or the company president, start with love and deliver on your promises. Your word is a promise to yourself and others. I know when I was growing up, I heard, "word is bond" a lot. That same principle still stands today. Your word is your bond. It is your work. It is your promise. Use your word to edify, love, and deliver consistently.

Be reliable

Reliability and gaining buy-in go hand and hand. The habit of reliability does not happen by doing something just once. Your reliability cannot be built from a promise only delivered once; it is your constant commitment to your verbal agreements that solidify your reliability. No matter how big or small something is. Building a habit of committing to the minuscule will help you develop the muscle to honor significant commitments with ease. Always remember, anything in life that is worth doing is worth overdoing.

Be on time

Reliability also ties into your physical presence. Another simple way of gaining buy-in from your peers is arriving at least 30 minutes early every day. Integrity, as Dr. Brené defines it, "is choosing what's right over what's fun, fast, or easy." I will be the first to say, arriving to work 30 minutes before I'm required to be there every day is not fun or easy.

For a year, I was committed to showing up for the people who worked with me. Over time, I knew I would be able to cash in on all of the hours of sleep I lost by adjusting my schedule. It sounds small, simple, and insignificant to many people, but I want you to test this out for yourself.

LEVEL-UP TIP:

The 30-minute Rule

Morning routines benefit our mental health and growth.
Some of the world's most successful women follow a morning routine to help them have a productive day, which ultimately leads to more wins throughout our day. Incorporate a 30-minute rule into your morning routine.

Being on time helps build a sense of security for the people who work with you. People can expect you to be at your desk/workspace, ready to work at the same time every day. This practice sends the message that you are unique and willing to go the extra mile for your peers and the people who directly work with you.

Be disciplined

Discipline is the strongest form of self-love. It is the single trait that says, "I am worth working hard for.", "My long-term goals are worth being uncomfortable for a short period of time.", "I love myself enough to go after the things I want in life." Discipline provides stability and structure to your life. It is an extremely marketable skill. Your ability to show up (literally) when the time arises adds that additional layer of trust. Discipline makes you unstoppable.

Own your narrative

One of the things that I have quickly learned in my professional career is that if you do not control your own story, others will create one for you. What do you genuinely want to be known for? Here are a few ways you can begin to take charge of your narrative:

- ✓ Speak up for yourself and learn the art of polite yet direct communication.

- ✓ Be solution-oriented. Be known as the problem solver, not the problem starter/complainer.

- ✓ Learn the art of balancing your light, power, and talent with authentic humility.

- ✓ Be brave. Own your mistakes quickly. Take steps towards correcting them even more rapidly.

As you sit at round tables, pitching ideas, remember the story you have painted around who you are as a professional. Are others confident in who you are and what you have to bring to the table? Are they buying what you are selling?

"Building a brand means knowing your story and building and sharing that story."

—*Tamara McCleary,*
Branding Expert, and Top Influencer
CEO of Thulium

CHAPTER 9

BOLD AND BRANDABLE

I wore many hats when I worked for the non-profit organization in Maryland. I found myself running around the office doing anything from cutting up strawberries for eager participants in training to programming telephones. Every day brought on its own set of challenges and, best of all, wins. I was grateful. We were a force. After two years of working there, I developed this «all-knowing» persona that was magnetic to the people who worked with me. They would call me for every little problem they had, and I would come to save them. My company believed in me and had confidence in the work I produced.

In many ways, this experience took me back to when I was a little girl and reminded me of the pride and responsibility I carried within myself, knowing my mother needed me to survive. I took pride in problem-solving in those offices filled with bright women. I can still hear the questioning tone in their voices speaker through my phone system, *"Um...Laura?"*. I always tried to respond with a sense of grace in my voice.

And so, the mantra *"Um...Laura?"* became the micro-culture that swirled the office. I became used to hearing it often. It was my brand. When I decided to leave the organization, the marketing director affectionately gifted me with a mug that read, *"Um...Laura?"* It was such a fun gift that would make me remember this team for lifetimes to come.

The mug wasn't the only reason why I would remember this organization. It was one of the most important roles I have ever held. It stretched me and taught me more than I could have ever learned anywhere else, in the shortest amount of time. This organization allowed me to establish an identity to begin to think about what I wanted out of a career and my own life.

LEVEL-UP TIP:

Establish a consistent and robust work identity.

Your workplace should recognize excellence when someone mentions your name, and as you walk through each door to sit at any table. Allow your light to shine; make yourself visible.

The women in that building were ahead of their time. I felt like we were always on an uphill battle to be innovative and establish ourselves as experts. The truth of the matter is, I have worked for many companies after I left this one and discovered we were not behind at all. We could get more done with fewer people and money than the big, more stabilized businesses. Like me, "my slap the table" boss also established a persona and brand for herself. She was introduced to you in Chapter 3 in a "not so pleasant" way, but truthfully, she let her passion get ahead of her only a few times. I truly adored her.

She was my first woman boss. She was unconditionally fierce in every sense of the word. She took conference calls from her elliptical. She would send emails at 3 AM and be in the office by 7 AM. She was a brilliant negotiator. She never took no for an answer. It was always more like an "I'll talk to you about it again at another time." She was persistent. I felt like she could get anything she wanted. And she was accomplished because of it.

Her ability to connect with others on an emotional level and her "stop at nothing" drive made her a unique leader. We went after huge federal grants despite being a small, boots on the ground type of business. She knew what we had to offer could compete with the big, more established organizations. Her business model was rooted in competition, and she knew supreme excellence was required to compete.

This fierce leader taught me to go after the things I wanted in life. She held us all to high standards and expected nothing but greatness. It was all tough love. It was all growing pains. I left the company because I felt like I learned everything I needed to learn in this role, but I would have worked with her forever.

LEVEL-UP TIP:

Negative branding is real and has consequences.

Establishing a negative brand is easy to do and takes a great deal of intentional effort to reverse. Be mindful of what you are known for.

Whether you are the enthusiastic all-knowing assistant or the fierce, passion-filled CEO, we all take on a persona. You are the face of your brand, so one of the first things you need to make sure of is that you are *visible*. If people do not see you, do not know you, then you do not exist in their world. Take a moment to reflect. What is your current work persona? Is it positive, negative, or non-impactful?

LEVEL-UP TIP:

Position yourself for leadership opportunities.

To be perceived as a competent leader, position yourself in your organization to be known and recognized for the things you would like to be known and recognized for. Remember, you are responsible for creating your own personal and professional narrative. If you don't, someone will surely create it for you.

As for my professional branding practice, I didn't mind running around putting out fires all day at the non-profit. I took great pride in it. I am sure my fierce boss also didn't mind that people sat up straight when she entered the room. She never told people to do that. We just did. If you don't want to be known for a bad attitude, laziness, or unreliability, then don't make that your brand.

You may have never dreamed of being an influencer. You might think it's a little cheesy. Although developing your brand at work is a lot like being an influencer, it requires time, buy-in, consistency, hard work, but most of all, it requires you to be present.

There are simple ways that you can begin to establish a presence at work. One of the ways I started was by volunteering for events. Any event that my company had, I was there, whether they were paying me to be there or not. Why? I knew I'd get a higher return just being present than actually getting paid to be there. People across the company would see my face more. I was viewed as "helpful," "flexible," "willing to pitch in," not because I was playing a part, but because that is who I am and what I strive to do more of. A few best practices can include the following;

- ✓ Ask a colleague that doesn't work in your department out to lunch.

- ✓ Put together, team builders.

- ✓ Don't be afraid to step out of your cubicle.

- ✓ Volunteer to serve on the Christmas Party committee.

- ✓ Ask your teammates what their biggest challenge is this week and how you can help them overcome them.

Everyone in the workforce could use a helping hand now and then or just a listening ear to bounce ideas off. What I want you to understand is helping others will ultimately serve you. In turn, you'll understand the organization's ins and outs on a deeper level and the barriers and challenges of others.

In Chapter 4, we discussed what it means to "find ways to say yes," I realize that "yes" isn't merely a three-letter word. Sometimes it can mean being present and flexible in a way that allows you to show up for others while serving yourself.

As you grow into your career, you will want to create what is called a personal brand. A personal brand can only develop through presence. Presence is the ultimate "yes."

CHAPTER 10

ZERO TALENT

Early on in my career, I found myself feeling unworthy of success. It was the *imposter syndrome* that would take over time and time again. Being a young brown girl brings on its own set of preconceived biases. Others may perceive you as spicy and feisty, oblivious and uneducated, or too sensual to be taken seriously. If you have never experienced this type of projection, you may never understand what it feels like to feel so unqualified for something because you don't fit the identity of a specific role in the workplace. Even though you know you are more qualified than the people sitting at the very same table as you.

It was refreshing to watch the documentary, "Becoming" on Netflix, where former first lady Michelle Obama shares highlighted moments from her life while promoting her book on tour.

Michelle says...

*"It's not just an image that we have; it's an image that we're given. People have told us, 'No, these are the things that aren't for you'...and I have been at, probably, every powerful table there is in the world. I've been at G-summits. I've been in castles and palaces, in boardrooms and academic universities. I am coming down from the mountaintop to tell every young person that is poor and working-class, and has been told, regardless of the color of your skin, that you don't belong, don't listen to them. **They don't even know how they got at those seats. They don't know.**"*

The audience roared as all of us, young and old, could relate to that feeling of inferiority. I walked into the breakroom of my part-time job one afternoon when I saw a poster that read, *Things That Require Zero Talent.*

Things that require ZERO TALENT:

Being on Time

Work Ethic

Effort

Body Language

Energy

Attitude
Passion
Being Coachable
Doing Extra
Being Prepared

(Original citation source unknown)

It wasn't fancy or anything. The poster was handwritten, and it appeared slightly aged as if the words were written and posted years ago when the store opened. The signage is likely a background fixture for their tenured employees, but I felt instantly inspired by the aesthetically worn, tried-and-true posting since I was new to the company. It was a small, part-time retail store where I worked to earn a few extra dollars on the side, and I couldn't help but consider how motivating and assuring the sign was. It was simple and applicable across all industries.

I consider myself a lifelong learner, so I am continually finding messages and learning opportunities in the most ordinary moments. The posting made me realize there will be moments in your career that will make you feel unqualified. Opportunities will come to you that make you feel unworthy. Please take a deep breath when those moments come and remember the beautiful qualities that you possess that require zero talent, like your ability to move and put out fires within an instance, your charm, resilience, and ability to be unapologetically graceful. The men who sit across from you in boardrooms might have more degrees than fingers and toes, but what you have that will always set you apart are the things that require zero talent. May you **never** let them outwork you.

"When you're following your inner voice, doors tend to eventually open for you, even if they mostly slam at first."

—*Kelly Cutrone*
American Publicist,
New York Times Best Selling Author,
and Television Personality

CHAPTER 11

CHALLENGING COLLABORATIONS

I have had many brilliant and powerful bosses in my lifetime. I have also worked with and have experienced challenges from many women and men who do not look like me. This feeling can be daunting, especially as a young person trying to get ahead in my career. When it comes to women, effective communication is something we find ourselves having to work twice as hard to overcome. Whether people don't understand our intentions or are just committed to misunderstanding us, communication barriers fall on us to resolve and overcome. In the famous words of Whitney Houston, "It's not right, but it's okay!"

As I have matured into higher career roles, I have come face to face with these challenges...

1. What do you say to your boss when they are wrong?

2. Can you call your boss out in the middle of a meeting?

3. What do you do when a colleague has an egregious plan or idea?

4. Do you go along with this plan and watch as the department goes up in flames?

LEVEL-UP TIP:

Communication is your personal responsibility.

Don't run from your personal responsibility to study communication best practices and apply specific communication needs to each working environment.

Challenging your superiors and work colleagues appropriately will demand more keen communication skills that will require you to dismantle any belief that women are too emotional or impulsive. Regardless of what anyone thinks, your opinions are valid in the workforce. Women often lean toward two positions regarding their views in the workforce;

1. Women either get too ahead of themselves and shove ideas down people's throats with no collaborative effort or regard.

2. We keep our excellent, valuable, exceptional opinions to ourselves.

The first instance usually occurs when women know and understand their power, and these women believe they are right regarding the circumstance at hand (by the way, most of the time, we are...but hey, I could be biased). The second behavior typically happens with women who struggle with *imposter syndrome*. These women don't think their views are worthy, and they are afraid of rejection.

If you believe that you fall into either one of these categories, don't worry, you are not alone. Although you may have never heard of the phrase "challenging appropriately" before today, it will save you from feeling grief and allow you to build strong collaborative relationships in the workforce. The best part of all is that it requires zero talent.

The next time you are at work and have an opposing idea, need to express an opinion or need to have an awkward conversation with a peer or superior, the primary internal questions that should come to mind are;

- ✓ *Is it the right place?*

- ✓ *Is this the right time?*

- ✓ *Is this my role/place?*

- ✓ *Is this the right person to communicate this to?*

☑ *Are my intentions pure?*

☑ *Is my ego in check?*

Be mindful by digging as deeply as possible within yourself when you are asking these questions. Be honest with yourself. The two ways we as women traditionally approach expressing ourselves should go out of the window.

Please understand that nobody is going to listen to someone they believe is out of control. This person will, in turn, lean into the belief that women are too unstable to make rational decisions. Sounds harsh, I know, but these are the subtle ways women of color can have our real power stripped away.

Nevertheless, if we continue not to share our opinions, this will inevitably take away our voices completely. Remaining silent detracts from your ability to be a collaborative team member. You have to start believing the truth of the matter; the workforce needs your voice.

Challenging appropriately starts with a few essential ingredients for success, including mutual respect, transparency, seeking understanding, open-mindedness, flexibility, and understanding nuance. Having mutual respect allows others to recognize a developing leader and hear their colleagues› perspectives before inserting their two cents. It also calls for the opposing party to listen to valuable concerns or what we have to contribute.

Transparency allows working professionals to put all

of their cards on the table. After all, if you are working with someone in the same company with a unified mission, chances are you have the same professional goals. Transparency allows for all parties to be aware of each other's intentions. Take a moment for self-reflection. Do you want to be right for the sake of being right, or do you want to truly be helpful?

If possible, attempt to seek understanding so that there will be a foundation of positionality established. Seek understanding to understand the facts of what you are challenging before you put your foot in your mouth. There is nothing worse than being loud and wrong. Remember, you are challenging the topic of belief, not the person. Challenges are not personal attacks in any way.

Being openminded and flexible allows us to let go of issues that aren't truly issues. Sometimes we have to be ready to let go, allow others to give things a shot, allow others to fail, express your opinions or concern, and be willing to bow out gracefully and support.

Lastly, understanding nuance means that there are gray areas to everything. Once you understand that two things can be true, you become more open to taking chances on what you are challenging.

LEVEL-UP TIP:

Learn to be okay with the gray.

Gray areas in life teach us that all experiences are not binary. Learning to understand nuances in perspectives and distinct differences in points of view make us more mature and ethical adults.

The ultimate goal is to be heard, collaborative, and to challenge everyone to be and do better. We all want others to like us, but we all want to be understood as well. The best thing to do is to challenge ourselves to challenge appropriately. So, put your gloves on, and be ready for the good fight.

"Choose your battles wisely. After all, life isn't measured by how many times you stood up to fight. It's not winning battles that makes you happy, but it's how many times you turned away and chose to look into a better direction. Life is too short to spend it on warring. Fight only the most, most, most important ones, let the rest go."

—C. JoyBell C.,
Author and Essayist
The Sun is Snowing (2014)

CHAPTER 12

THE GOOD FIGHT

A s a woman of color, you are likely to experience certain biases within the workforce day-in and day-out. There is a strong possibility that there will be people who don't want you to succeed. You will likely have employees who challenge your authority and peers who steal your innovative ideas and sell them like their own. This chapter will help you better manage the interpersonal exchanges at work that are worth your energy and time.

We all know this practice will require strategic balance, and to be effective at choosing our battles, we must learn to be cautious regarding what we allow to let eat-us-up or disturb our peace. I say *choose* because you can decide what consumes your energy.

Let's try this short exercise:

Close your eyes for 5 seconds.

Now picture a red bear.

Now imagine a red bear in your bedroom.

Now open your eyes.

Were you able to successfully imagine the red bear in your bedroom? If so, then this is proof that you can control your thoughts. Now that you are aware that you have the power to control your thoughts, you can also control, regulate, and redirect where you put your energy.

LEVEL-UP TIP:

Get ahold of your thinking.

Women who lead do not allow their minds to run aimlessly. These women understand that their brains are a machine that can be programmed, updated, and refreshed whenever they choose. As Eckhart Tolle says, "You are not your thoughts. You have thoughts." Don't let your thoughts 'have' you.

You might be thinking to yourself, "No, some people just get on my nerves" or "Uh, uh, some people have to know their place." You are correct! I am here to tell you that healthy conflict is appropriate in the workplace if it falls into this one simple concept; Whatever point you are arguing has to add value to both parties, not just yourself. If whatever you have to say or whatever you want to do is not beneficial, perpetuates a disagreement, or reinforces your desire to be right, you are better off walking away from it. If you cannot help the situation, at least don't hurt the situation or make it worse.

I have spent way too many hours on issues that were either not that important or just for the sake of what we refer to as "the principle." "It's just the principle." Well, my new philosophy is to *get over it* unless you can have an edifying conversation with the person you are working with to seek understanding and bring some resolve. If you cannot, then seriously, let it go. Here are a few things to look out for when choosing your battles wisely;

Do not allow others to take your kindness for weakness
I am not instructing you to walk away from every hard conversation there is. It requires the opposite of you. It is the way we handle these situations that differentiates between the winners and the losers. Look for the win-win in situations. Strive to let people know how you feel regarding work performance, expectations, and general

boundaries for respect in the workplace without attacking insignificant battles that focus on small, often hypothetical scenarios.

Be supportive to your peers, whether you like them on a personal level or not

Try to make yourself available to be supportive. We have to recognize that some people are self-righteous in their stupidity. If we were to be completely vulnerable with ourselves, I am sure there are times when each of us has been bullheaded and steadfast and utterly wrong. I can name a few times early on in my career where I was stuck-on-stupid. Some people need all the support they can get even if they make bad choices or go about things the wrong way.

This principle also applies to how you interact with your boss. Remember, your boss, your direct workplace authority figure, and your immediate leadership reference, in the best cases, made it into their role for a reason. Whether you agree on their competence level, it is in your best interest that you invest in this relationship as much as possible. You don't want to cause a tense relationship between you and your leadership. Instead, you want to cultivate and nourish this connection so that when there is a battle (and trust me, there will always be a battle of some sort), others won't see you as an adversary, but rather a concerned ally.

Learn to have hard conversations when you are less emotional about them

It is ok to have a "cooling-off" period to collect your thoughts and gather solid rational examples for your argument. As you become comfortable addressing conflict with respect, you will ultimately find there is no need for substantial emotional investment. This will save you a lot of time and energy.

Ground yourself

You don't know everything, and sometimes you have to let go and let people fail or watch them win. Be open to feedback and new experiences. All experiences, challenges, and direct conflict do not require your immediate input. Step aside and occasionally observe, especially if you are new to your position and you are still learning your coworkers' personalities. Either way, if you take the right stance, you will either be there to catch them when they fall or drink sparkling cider when they win.

Determine which battles you are willing to take, when to stop challenging and surrender, and when to keep pressing forward. Don't pressure yourself if you don't get it right the first time. This is a journey, not a sprint. Keep moving towards your goal of perfecting healthy conflict resolution skills, knowing when to step away, and protecting your light.

"I will not be another flower, picked for my beauty and left to die. I will be wild, difficult to find, and impossible to forget."

—*Erin Van Vuren,*
Poet and Modern Intellectual
Founder of PaperCrumbs

CHAPTER 13

RESISTING RESILIENCE

I was running frantically up and down the hallways of my job one Monday morning listening to my boss lecture me about my recent huge, yet fixable mistake. I was the coordinator for our annual national training session that brought twenty eager experts from across the country to enhance their growing expertise. It was a big deal for our organization, and I took pride in making sure this week went on without a hitch. Unfortunately, I was already off to a lousy start that morning as the facilitator marched into my office with her lips pressed tightly to not let on to how upset she was. It turns out I printed hundreds and hundreds of documents she needed for the week-long program incorrectly.

> ### LEVEL-UP TIP:
>
> ## Own your mistakes
>
> Mistakes happen. Own them quickly; address them accurately.

We shared an exchange that ultimately ended in her making me feel like I had no idea what I was doing. I was the lead coordinator for this event for the past two years. It was one of those projects I dreaded once it came around, and yet I got a strong sense of fulfillment after accomplishing it and making it better every year. Naturally, her words stung me and shook my confidence and sense of awareness. Of course, I knew what I was doing. I had done this training many times, and yet I couldn't shake the embarrassment I felt. I scurried around, trying to right my wrongs as one of the newer facilitators gave me a genuine nudge of encouragement. She stopped me dead in my tracks and said, "I admire your resilience."

Her well-meaning words hit me like a sudden overpowering wind. Her words intended for kindness and empowerment only made me want to retreat to my office and scream. I know I am strong and powerful beyond measure, but I felt vulnerable and threatened.

It has been years since this incident, and yet I still carry it with me. It has made me chant the word "resilience" in my subconscious like a mantra, piercing me every time I think of it. Women of color tend to hear the word "resilience" more often than our counterparts, and in the heat of my frustration, it offended me and felt like a purgatory of sorts.

As young women of color, our strengths are often measured by how much pain we can endure. This ultimately means we are consistently put to the test, whether purposefully or not, and it is a stringent societal norm to challenge. The world tells us to hold our heads high in the face of disappointment, and countless other well-meaning, yet ultimately oppressing phrases like;

> *"Don't you dare cry in front of a crowd."*

> *"You can only express defeat in the comfort of your loved ones with whom you can show your vulnerability."*

> *"You must be both strong and feminine."*

> *"You must be all things."*

Learning the boundaries to your resilience is self-love and doesn't require talent. As much as we like to think our body is a time-traveling machine with an extended service plan, it is simply not true. You can only be in one place at one time, and if you are sick or your mental health is not in a great place, you have to make time for yourself to heal. *It is okay to have an awful day.*

Have you ever had one of those, "I'm going to update my resume" type of days? The ones where you start searching Indeed for anything in your current salary range and role. I can determine how bad a day I've had by how long I search for a new job. It's funny but true, and we have all been there. I want you to know it's okay. You are human, but just remember it's just a day. One hard conversation. One mistake. One disappointment. One day. Feel your feelings – you can even scream if you need to, but don't let self-pity stay in your body too long. You are worth more than just one awful day. Hit the reset when you need a break and come back strong.

Listen to your body
Please listen to your body. Be present every single day so that you will notice when your body becomes ill. Strive to achieve optimal mental and physical wellness. How can you be any good for anyone else if you are barely hanging on to yourself?

Avoid negative self-talk
You don't have to be a superhero or wear a cape to embody resilience. Some thinking patterns are simply untrue, and once you stop believing them, you will stop feeding them. I saw a story online one day that read…

> *An old Cherokee is teaching his grandson about life. "A fight is going on inside me," he said to*

the boy. "It is a terrible fight, and it is between two wolves. One is evil — he is anger, envy, sorrow, regret, greed, arrogance, self- pity, guilt, resentment, inferiority, lies, false pride, superiority, and ego." He continued, "The other is good — he is joy, peace, love, hope, serenity, humility, kindness, benevolence, empathy, generosity, truth, compassion, and faith. The same fight is going on inside you — and every other person too." The grandson thought about it for a minute and then asked his grandfather, "Which wolf will win?" The old Cherokee simply replied...

"The one you feed."

We have already proven in Chapter 13 you can control your thoughts. Once you stop feeding the negative feelings you have about yourself, you will starve those thoughts, and those thoughts will eventually pass. The story you create in your mind will project onto other people and everything you do. If you don't love yourself, take yourself seriously, or take genuine pride in your work, who will?

LEVEL-UP TIP:

Self-love is a direction, not an option.

Self-love is not a luxury or an option. It is a necessary component for effective leadership and healthy life governance.

Walk in gratitude

You work really hard. Be gracious to others and, most importantly, yourself. Be thankful that you are able-bodied. You have a strong mind. Appreciate your ability to be anything you want in this world and don't take your life and what you have worked for granted. Don't underestimate your journey. Even if it feels small. A little goes a long way.

Do not run yourself into a hole, trying to be everyone's saving grace. Most importantly, do not feel guilty for not being able to help everyone. Even if that person is yourself. You have the right to take breaks. You can get up and stand tall after you have fallen. You can recover from any downfall. Do not let your resilience become an all-consuming compulsion that ultimately leads you down a path of burnout and destruction.

"If they don't give you a seat at the table, bring a folding chair."

—*Shirley Chisholm,*
American Politician and Activist
The first African American woman to be elected to U.S.
Congress, representing New York's 12th congressional
district from 1969-1983, a total of seven terms.

CHAPTER 14

SORRY, NOT SORRY

I sat at an all-staff meeting on a Friday morning for our company updates. We typically have a popcorn approach for updates where each department head shares their weekly update. The director went one by one, selecting each department to speak. As updates were coming to an end, I noticed he skipped over the employee performance department. This just so happened to be MY department. My colleague, a Black man, head of Engineering, noticed that the director skipped my turn to share updates. My colleague kicked me under the table a few times, urging me to say something, but I didn't say anything. I let the meeting conclude without a peep from me.

As excited as I was to share my accomplishments this week and all the innovative things in store for our company's performance programming, I could feel my light leave my body. It is a weird feeling to be forgotten in the workplace.

Women of color often struggle with two different yet interestingly intertwined experiences within the workplace. We are either hyper-visible or utterly invisible to our counterparts.

Being hyper-visible is the environment that others create around our bodies, what we wear, the way we talk. We are often pegged as too curvy in some of the most unflattering clothing or too loud when having opposing views. Our passions become stereotypes of the *feisty Latina*, and of course, the *angry Black woman*.

Being invisible is another, in my opinion, more heart-shattering struggle black and brown women face in the workforce. When people forget to acknowledge us in meetings, when people forget our names, when people call us another person of color's name, or when someone takes our hard work from us, and someone else is given credit for it.

My colleague walked with me out of the conference room that morning and with a stern look on his face. His eyes could have pierced me as he told me, "Never put yourself on the back burner." I replied and said, "I didn't really have anything important to say.", but he pushed right past my excuses. He shot back, "Sure, you did. Never let them put you on the back burner again." I guess making an excuse for it felt better than acknowledging I was completely ignored and invisible to the director.

I'm tired, and I know you are too. Although we don't make up many of the leadership roles in our organizations, I know we want to, we have worked hard, and we are more than qualified to lead with skill and competence. I want to encourage you to start being unapologetically you...

You in all your expertise.

You in all your wisdom.

You in all your grace.

You in all your passion.

Do not let them quiet your voice. Do not let them dim your light, exaggerate your views, or make you invisible. Do not let them box you into those stereotypes.

Everything I have shared with you up to this point should be executed unapologetically in your own right and with poise. There are ethical rules for getting ahead, yet no one prepares us for the challenges we will inevitably face. Women of color even use apologetic language in our daily speech. We use it unknowingly to appease and essentially ask others for permission to do our job.

Here are a few simple tips to take a step into executing your role unapologetically:

Never put yourself on the backburner

Delivering messages with apologetic undertones is a way of putting yourself on the back burner. We often do this by saying things like, "I'll be quick." or "It's not really *that* important.". These are ways that we diminish our own messages. *"There's nothing enlightened about shrinking so that other people won't feel insecure around you."* What you have to share for the greater good of the group is essential to the business. If it were not essential, you wouldn't be asked to speak in the first place.

Avoid "sorry" gestures

Women often use a lot of social pleasantries and habitually apologize even when we haven't done anything wrong. Sometimes we might physically shrink ourselves and walk with our heads down to avoid eye contact. When we are trying to get by someone, we tend to say, "sorry, excuse me" when there is no reason to be "sorry." Pay close attention to the ways you might be bringing on an apologetic aura to yourself. Let go of that sentiment and lead with confidence.

Don't ask for permission to execute

There was a time in my career that I would email my boss for permission to sneeze. I'm obviously kidding, but that is what I realized it was like. I would constantly seek permission to do a job I was hired to do. Our actions shape the way people view us. Since my boss knew I could not make a decision without her blessing, she perpetuated that sentiment for years to come. After years of me inviting this behavior to myself, of course, when I didn't openly share or ask for permission for certain things, she felt slighted.

When you are hired for a role, don't be afraid to execute what you know is best. There is nothing wrong with taking partnerships or a collaborative approach to decision making, but once you start building an identity around dependency, you will live in a world that requires you to ask for permission and feel sorry when you don't.

Eliminate the word "just" from your speech (including emails)

Your words are precious. Using the word "just" in emails tends to minimize what you are trying to accomplish or what you have accomplished. For example, saying, "I'm just wondering." or "I'm just letting you know" takes away your authority. Instead, what you are seeking is the ability to exude confidence. Using the word "just" dilutes and reduces the space for what you are really trying to communicate.

We, black and brown women, are part of the most educated group in the United States. Yet somehow, we encounter the most barriers towards economic advancement and are expected to work harder than our counterparts. If you are reading this book, it is likely that you, similar to me, are over it!

When I lived in Maryland, I visited my brother's friend and his wife for dinner. We sat around the table talking about Virginia and adjusting to being in Maryland, specifically Baltimore. His wife angled her body towards me and stared into my eyes. She said, "be careful." I was 18 years old at the time, and although it was a short, intense stare-off of sorts, it stayed with me.

I was repeatedly told as a young adult, "Take care of yourself." I didn't quite understand what that meant until I entered the real world, the workforce. Today, "Take care of yourself" holds a whole new meaning. It means to "protect yourself," mind, body, and soul—both professionally and personally.

I thank God every day for the allies he has brought to me throughout the years. They have used their power as a microphone to amplify my voice, but I still have a tremendous amount of work to do for myself and others. Like my colleague, a black male, who threatened me into not settling, I appreciate his feedback because he recognizes the importance of not allowing what occurred to happen again.

As former United States President Barack Obama said in one of his early speeches, "A rising tide lifts all boats." to which Angela Rye graciously refuted by saying, "Not everyone has a boat." There are so many of us out there who don't have the tools or don't even know where to start. This book represents your guide to grabbing a boat. For me, it began with Mrs. Erica. For you, it might start with this book. For someone else, it will begin with you.

Always remember success is to be taken. Nobody owes us anything more than the value we bring. The workforce is a difficult place for us to shine and thrive, so we must create spaces for ourselves and our sisters to be unapologetically successful.

"Then I realized I wanted to write a love letter to women of color. I needed to take advantage of this opportunity to tell our stories and shine a light on the fact that not all women experience the workplace in the same way.

—Minda Harts,
American Author and Professor at New York University
The Memo: What Women of Color Need to Know to Secure a Seat at The Table (2019)

DEFINITIONS

As defined by Merriam-Webster, Dictionary.com, and personal editorial reflection.

Accountability

Noun

1. Is the state of being accountable, especially in terms of *personal accountability.*

1. Accountability is often discussed with transparency and consequences. This typically involved keeping people and organizations accountable by making their actions *visible* and having consequences when those actions are not acceptable.

Boundaries

Noun

1. Something that indicates the farthest limit.

2. An emotional, psychological, spiritual, or physical line of division for access from undesired external, or at times, internal experiences.

Buy-In

Noun

1. Acceptance of and willingness to actively support and participate in something such as a proposed new plan, policy, or even belief in someone's ability to accomplish goals at hand.

Compromise

Noun

1. An agreement or a settlement of a dispute that is reached by each side making concessions

Collaboration

Noun

1. The action of working with someone to produce or create something.

Ego

Noun

1. A person's sense of self-esteem or self-importance.

2. The part of the mind that mediates between the conscious and the unconscious and its responsible for reality testing and a sense of personal identity.

Entitlement

Noun

1. The amount to which a person has a right.

2. The belief that one is inherently deserving of privileges or special treatment.

Grace

Noun

1. Allowed room and space for improvement, growth, and redemption after conscious or unconscious error, poor decision making, or mishandling of situations, things, and events.

Hypervisibility (in the workplace)

Noun

1. The state of being able to see or be seen

2. The extreme or exaggerated perceived presence of Black and Brown women within professional workspaces; heightened sensitivity to all words, actions, and at times non-actions of this subgroup.

Intentional

Adjective

1. Done on purpose; deliberate.

2. Conscious

3. Holistically aware of decided upon thoughts and how these thoughts translate into action

Invisibility (in the workplace)

Noun

1. Inability to be seen.

2. The state of being ignored or not taken into consideration.

3. The extreme or exaggerated lack of acknowledgment of Black and Brown women within professional

workspaces; heightened insensitivity to all words, actions, and at times non-actions of this subgroup, resulting in being dismissed and ignored.

Imposter Syndrome

Noun

1.   The persistent inability to believe that one's success is deserved or has been legitimately achieved as a result of one's efforts or skills; see: A LIE

People Pleaser

Noun

1.   A person who has an emotional need to please others often at the expense of his or her own needs or desires

Influencer (in professional spaces)

Noun

1.   A person or thing that influences another

2.   A person with the ability to influence the energetic atmosphere of their workplace and adjust it to their desired outcome.

Intuitive

Adjective

1.   A feeling of knowing based on what one feels to be true even without conscious reasoning.

Self-betrayal

Noun

1.   The intentional or inadvertent revelation of the truth about one's actions or thoughts.

Shrinking

Adjective

1. Becoming smaller in size or amount.

   Verb

1. The act of diminishing one's talents and skills to accommodate the personalities of your workplace, either due to influences of external or, at times, internal insecurities.

Solution-Oriented

Adjective

1. The ability to see situations, events, experiences, thoughts, and perceived problems through a lens that aims to develop an optimistic answer to the aforementioned occurrences.

Victim Mentality

Adjective

1. An acquired personality trait in which a person tends to recognize or consider themselves at a disadvantage due to others' negative actions; not to be confused with the state of being psychologically or physically abused, in which a person is, in reality, a victim.

2. A mental state that the world is against you and that there is no opportunity for growth, hope, or moving beyond unpleasant experiences.

EPILOGUE

I wrote this book in hopes that people who looked like me would have a source for professional development. Quite frankly, I was tired of reading leadership books from men and women who could not relate to us. Here are a few statistics that propelled me to my professional development journey and inspired me to create a product that would serve and prepare a highly ignored demographic, Black, and Brown women.

Over 38% of millennials compose our workforce today, as quoted by CNBC (2019). Of this 38%, over 47% are women, and more notably, 38% of this group are Women of Color, according to Forbes (2019). After realizing this, I knew that it was time for someone to start writing to and for us as we aim to advance our professional careers. We need to start demanding that "seat at the table" that we so are worthy of and desperately deserve.

Some people will side-eye and subtly tell you that you will never be successful with the principles I have outlined. But let me make a viable point clear- those people do not know you. You would not have purchased this book and made it this far in your dreams without knowing you were capable. They don't know where you came from to get the role you currently have. They don't know that nothing will stop you.

I know our stories are so vastly different. We are not a monolithic group by any means. Our careers started at different points in our lives. You may not have grown up teaching your mother how to spell. You might already be making six-figures as a young millennial in the workforce. You might be thinking of quitting your job or going into a new field. No matter where you are right now in your career, I know some days can be challenging, and when those days arise, I want you to think of this book and the many ways you are a power, a force, and light. You don't need a Ph.D. to stand out. You don't need a three-piece suit for others to take you seriously. You don't need to bury your history and background deep down inside of you. You don't need to make yourself invisible when an authority walks into the room.

Remember to learn from your missed opportunities, listen to the people you admire, stay strong in your "yes" and firm in your "no's." You are not just lucky. Your success didn't happen by accident. Never forget that there are ten simple, 100% doable things you can do that require ZERO talent. Write it down, post it up, and remind yourself that you are valuable just the way you are. This is not science, nor do I have the final say for what works for women of color in the workforce. I am only here to give expert analysis on what has worked for me and how I have garnered a salary that is more than 25% of the average 30-year-old woman in the workforce.

I am telling you what is practical, which has always been the most important thing to me. I don't want young women to feel like they need to dumb themselves down, be more docile, apologetic, accommodating, or invisible. I want the women that I know to stand firm in their decision making and use what we already have as our power.

Because what you have is....

Incredibly unique.

Incredibly bright.

Incredibly passionate.

Incredibly a woman.

Incredibly made.

Incredibly powerful.

Incredibly *visible*.

ACKNOWLEDGMENTS

When I told my mother I was writing a book, she was so overwhelmed and intrigued. "How long have you been working on this? 5 years?" I laughed a good belly laugh. "No, mommy," I said. "More like 7 months." Mommy, I want to thank you for your inquisitive nature. Your only baby girl is accomplishing things beyond your wildest dreams, and quite frankly mine as well.

My grandmother, my saving grace, you are so poetic and have shown me how to move through life with poise and dignity.

My two brothers, Roberto and Luis, you gave me an adventurous childhood. You are the reason I'm not afraid of getting dirty, and I'm not "too good" for any job on the planet. Well, except for taking out the trash. Mommy said that's your job.

Irene Raudales, through thick and thin girl. If I moved to Mars, you would find a way to talk to me. To say I love you would be a disservice.

Kaylannie, you taught me everything I know and supported every one of my crazy ideas. If I wanted to be a coconut, you'd find me a palm tree. Thank you for your unconditional love.

Kristen Owens, Ashley Adkinson, Lajeesa Teague, also known as "The Squaddd." Although we have known each other for over 15 years, you always manage to find a way to support me and show up for me. Whether I am having a birthday, going through a breakup, or writing a book, you all have always had my back. You always cheer me on and gas me up. You always remind me that I am a force. I am so proud to have such a witty, fun, and smart group of powerful women to call my friends.

My colleague, Ty, you are a giant, and you shouldn't have to, but you watch your step when you walk in the room to not step on others. Your brilliance and professionalism won't allow me to forget what I am worth. Thank you for using your power to elevate women in the workforce. It is men like you who make room for women like me.

My employees, I have learned so much being your leader. This year has been rough for many families and the workforce. Thank you for staying dedicated to your role, supporting others over yourself, and showing up and showing out every day! You are indeed my rock stars. I could never be a great leader without your collaboration.

My "Big" sister, Sydney Golden, thank you for working with me through the years to make my dreams come true, and always checking in and making a way to spend time with me outside of our projects. I appreciate your friendship.

Cydni M. Robertson, my Editor, it was imperative for me to work with women of color for this project, so it was such a pleasure to work with you. You had excellent ideas for *Visible*, and I was so pleased to incorporate them to take *Visible* to the next level. Thank you!

Kedi Darby, my graphic designer, thank you for your work on the cover. Your work will help me market *Visible* to the masses.

My launch team who pulled their resources together to put this book in the best position for success. I always tell people how precious time is. It is the one resource we can never get back. When someone dedicates their time to something, it is because it is important to them. Thank you, Marlisa Sanders, La'Keia Brown, DHA, Amanda Nicole Thompson, MAOL, Abel Ramirez, Fulvia Palma-Alvelo, and TeVeira Hillyer. You didn't have to dedicate any time to this book, but you did, and I am forever grateful for your love and support.

My extended friends and family, any release I have, whether from The Writing Shop, a blog, an article, or a book, you patiently wait behind the curtains to bow with me. Thank you for buying from my store, sharing my work around the world, and celebrating my life's most precious moments with me.

I assure you this list was not completed in any order, and if I forgot to mention you specifically, blame it on my head and not my heart. There are countless of you around the world who have cheered me on and sent me messages just to check-in. Even in my darkest hours, you stayed with me. This year has been challenging for many of us. There were many days I was not up for much conversation, and you weren't offended, and you loved me through it.

It is with much gratitude that I release my very first book. I am humbled by the experience. I hope this book made and created for us continues to evolve into something greater. That we might have a better understanding of who we are, the power we harness, and how to unleash that power.

www.ingramcontent.com/pod-product-compliance
Lightning Source LLC
Chambersburg PA
CBHW022043190326
41520CB00008B/692